BLIND FOLDED

BRANDY SIMMONS

Contents

Introduction

Growing in my spirituality has been an adventure that has had many twists and turns. I've always been curious concerning the mysteries of God. As I grew into my teenage years and into a young adult, I've had the opportunity to experience many different facets of church but always knew there was so much more I wanted to experience. That "much more" was living an abundant life. After many failed relationships whether friends or marriage, God and his compassion begin to show me what I had been longing for ever since I decided to "give my life to him". In this book, I will be sharing some of my journal entries, some of my stories, triumphs and how God carried me through the darkness and into the beginning of my abundant life.

Acknowledgements

This book is dedicated to all my universal guides. To the loves of my life, my gifts, my children, Israel, Lauryn, and Madisyn, you are my blessings from the Most High and I'm so grateful to be your mother.

To my mother Enonas Lewis, niece Crystal King and nephew Carsen Heirs, my late grandmother Gladys Timmons, aunts and uncles, thank you for being my support system. To my late father James Charles, I honor you and know that you are watching over me.

To my extended family/friends/sisters thank you for your consistency and love throughout this journey. You all mean everything to me.

This journey through my life will inspire you, expand a new perspective of your spiritual journey, and open you up to explore where God desires to take you individually as you trust his guidance. I've opened space for you to share your reflections as you read through the chapters.

As you begin to write, my prayer is that God would speak to you and give you clarity and comfort along your journey with him.

CHAPTER 1

It Started in The Dark

When I got the idea to write this book, it was during one of the longest, darkest seasons of my life. I must acknowledge that most of this journey came because of my own decision making for my life and what I thought was good for me. I knew that what I was going through was not just for me but would be a guide for individuals all over the world. The level of testing that I had to endure during that season was beyond what I could've never imagined.

I was on my way to encountering God in a most interesting way. Fear joined me on this journey and was committed to sticking by my side as long as I allowed it. It was fear of the unknown, fear of losing everything and not recovering from it, fear of not being protected, the fear of lack and anything else I could think of. At the end of all that negativity, I knew without a doubt that God was the ultimate genius, and my masterful guide in everything I was going to encounter in this life. Easier said than done right? Even in my resistance to the process, everything in me wanted God's best for me. I had to allow God to lead me and lead me without giving me all the details. Even though my trust for God was challenged, I wasn't crazy enough to severe my connection with him. God was all

I had, I could have chosen other options but common sense told me to stick with God. I needed him no matter how frustrated I was, no matter how angry and confused I was. I had to constantly go back and remember how he carried me through my childhood, through school, while struggling with my identity, when I didn't value me nor honor myself the way that I should have, God in all his bountiful mercy and love never saw me as a mistake and continued to remind me of that. Deep down in my soul, I knew God was never going to desert me and unlike previous years, this time around, I couldn't take matters into my hands. I had to relinquish all my power and control to him.

Throughout this book, I'm going to be sharing some of my personal journal entries that were written over time during my journey with God.

Tho the journey is not complete, and there will be more testimonies to share, I wanted to get all of you started on the appetizer. Here we go! I remember singing a song in church called, "I Surrender All". All to Jesus, I surrender, all to him I freely give. I will ever love and trust him in his presence daily live." I took a moment to reflect on those lyrics, I began to realize that I was not committed to surrendering anything. I failed, many times at my own commitment in allowing God to have free reign of my life. I just didn't know how to do it and in many ways, I desired to have control of my own life. When the pressure was on, nothing could wait, I had to take action.

I've always had a deep connection with God in that I always felt free to talk to him about any and everything. When I sung songs, I knew he could feel the sentiments of my heart. The groanings of my soul and spirit, only he could understand the depth of them. There were heartfelt prayers I had prayed, yearning to know him more, to discover the God that was in me, even when I couldn't articulate it, he knew all my desires.

He was about to show me what true surrender was, and I was not 100% ready for it.

Reflections

CHAPTER 2

Peeling Back the Layers

The year 2002 I graduated from college. June of that year, I went through a painful separation from an organization that left me confused about Christianity, God and myself. By July, I was in a new organization and by December, married and several years later with three children.

I was walking through life aware that I was not okay but never had the words to describe it and didn't have the courage to go get professional help for my trauma. Have you ever been in a place in your life where you knew you loved God, you were trying to do things with character and integrity and it seemed like the fruit of your labor was fire and brimstone?

After thirteen years of serving in the last organization, me and my family left.

I understood our departure to be that we had grown as much as we could there. Without asking a lot of questions I followed suit. I was relieved, elated to step into something new but without a hint of where we were going. I finally had my family and thought we could finally spend more time together and experience the world we seemed to be secluded from.

It felt good to wake up on Sundays and not have to prepare for services.

What I thought was light at the end of the tunnel became a complete nightmare. I had no clue of how the layers of my life would begin unraveling.

I realized quickly that my marriage was woven tightly into other things more than it should have been. When we had marital challenges, church was our escape, there were rare moments we took to deal with where we were together. Now that we were out of the church, there was nowhere else to turn but to ourselves. While I was home making memories with my children, my husband found an escape into the lives of other individuals that kept him occupied more outside of the home than in. He became a counselor to everyone that was transitioning out of that organization and never took time to come together with me to repair our own house. There were several deeply hurt people, but I knew it wasn't our place to do God's job. There was a ticking time bomb about to go off and I had no idea that it was happening. I wanted no parts of it and wanted to move in peace, but it seemed like the worst was headed directly towards me. Only God knew the depths of what was going on, better than anybody else. My desires had come to a screeching halt, I had enough of the whole church experience.

More and more the layers started peeling back right before my eyes.

God begin exposing more of my marriage. What was being exposed was shocking and heartbreaking. Prior to my family's departure I was excused of having an affair that never happened and my husband insisted that I go before the leaders to give them details. While I was being interrogated, he did not willingly share what was really happening in the life he was secretly living. Some years later the guy that I had been accused of being with sent me a DM apologizing for lying on me and wished the best for my life. I never responded back and continued to move through the process.

I asked God, "why me, I didn't ask for this!" It seemed like the more drama I had experienced; the more I pulled myself away from God's presence.

I stopped praying, reading the bible, I was angry and frustrated because I couldn't understand what was happening to my life.

It was never supposed to be this way. I wanted someone to explain to me why my faith and service to God was back firing on me. It felt like I had been cursed. No matter how much I wanted to explain my situation to someone, I knew they wouldn't understand or have a clue to what I was feeling. There was a disconnect between me and God, I had put someone and something in his place. This felt way different than what I had experienced before. To gain a fresh start I decided that me and my children could began visiting other organizations in another town, surely that would help comfort me. I thought this would help get me in a better space mentally.

The more I visited these different organizations, the more I felt like I was sinking into a bigger hole with no way out. I couldn't hear anything, couldn't feel anything, I was in complete despair, this wonderful dream I had envisioned was shattering. I remember one day arriving to church, deeply depressed. I took my kids into children's church and proceeded to go into the adult worship service. As I walked in, I wanted to drop to the floor, I wanted to scream out for help, I was hoping that someone could see (spiritually) my desperate plea for help. Surely there was someone in this big church spiritual enough to feel that something wasn't right with me. I wanted to know what to do to escape this madness that was happening to me. I stayed and sat in service with tears streaming down my face. I knew by the end of the service, nothing was going to change. I found myself riding back home in more tears knowing I was headed back to a place that I had no desire to be anymore.

Reflections

CHAPTER 3

Standing For Justice

The year 2015 to year 2017 I became numb to everything. These were the loneliest days of my life. I left a job of thirteen years and began fighting a situation that I knew was unfair and not justifiable. This went on for almost three years. My husband didn't support how I handled the situation, nevertheless I went forward with what I knew was right. No matter what people thought about me, I knew I didn't have the time to convince anyone that God had me in my current position.

This was the first time in my life needing government assistance. I was thankful because God was showing me through that entire ordeal that he was my source and no man could do what he needed to do for me. The ordeal with my former job finally came to an end and God made all things work in my favor. I knew that I owed that fight to myself. I was proud of me.

Within this timeframe, there was what felt like a deep ripping away of my marriage and it began to feel extremely toxic. Constant infidelity, my name being trashed to other people, and a cold heart is what I was experiencing. It felt like someone was constantly taking a knife and stabbing me in my heart.

I've never felt pain sting like this before. There was a moment when I wanted attention and briefly engaged this extremely attractive guy in the military, we would talk on the phone periodically until he asked me to come to his home. I knew then that had to stop, and I went completely ghost. In all the hurt I was experiencing, even though doing what was done to me may have felt deserving, I was faithful to God first. I then later told my husband about what had occurred because it was the right thing to do and the response was, "that's on me". The more I tried to express my pain to him, the more it felt like I was talking to a brick wall. The idea of marriage counseling was not considered so I took a step into getting my own therapy.

As I continued with therapy and continued to write in my journal, I knew at some point I would have to be vulnerable enough to share my journal entries in hopes that it would help someone on their path of getting free from whatever they were afraid to leave for their own good and the good of their children. By the year 2018 I was beyond tired and knew I did not want to spend another year doing what I had done before. I began rising out of the dark place. God was getting me prepared for what I was about to walk into next.

God began to expose the affair that was going to provide me with favor that I never expected. He was taking me to meet her face to face. He sent me to a temporary job where she was already employed. She knew exactly who I was before I knew who she was.

Not too long after leaving that job, all the pieces were getting ready to come together for me. I had been having several dreams about my marriage and the condition that it was in. I wanted to stick it out because I was told changes would be made, things were going to get better, so he said, but he began to get really sloppy with cleaning up his evidence.

January of 2019 God began sending me messages from people that had no idea the severity of my marriage, I received messages from another state that had information about my husbands' affairs, people were having prophetic dreams about the condition of my husband's heart and I had my own raw evidence. I remember having a conversation with God a couple of years before things got out of control. He spoke to me and said that this decision to leave would be solely up to me. He gave me the power to choose. I think this is a great space to talk about how people like to pray us through marriages that are completely dead. Many don't mean any harm by praying, but when you know firsthand, the condition of your house and how it is breaking you down, thank them for the prayers and respectfully move forward in seeking God for direction on what to do for your well-being.

When you are in an abusive, toxic relationship, you've got to know that this is not God's best for you, male or female. When you decide to make the decision to move forward, you've got to, as much as possible keep your own nose clean to receive the blessing of the Lord. Don't do people the way they've done you. No matter how justified you feel in doing it, know that you must be accountable and faithful to God, first.

Let people say what they will. The ones that will do the most talking haven't stepped foot in your home a whole day to know what you've had to endure.

You remain unmovable.

Reflections

CHAPTER 4

Take control of what I can control

I had to find ways to bring positive energy into my space and in my mind while this open affair happened before my eyes. I watched the mistress post on social media subliminal messages about how she was in love with my husband and trying to give others marital advice. She knew I was watching.

We were still social media friends since we began working together in 2018 up until my husband surprisingly was served his divorce papers. This particular affair gave me what I needed to end one of longest books of my life. While going through the divorce, they had done a relationship seminar together and sat on several christian panels together speaking on concerns of the church. This was disheartening to watch because some of the recipients did not know who they had speaking into their lives. I had to watch trips being taken, see him come home and not utter a word to him of what I knew. I was committed to my assignment and was going to complete it by any means necessary. Journal entry March 27, 2019, "Today I forced myself out of a slump. I've gone back to one of my favorite and productive activities, exercising. I had forgotten how great I feel after doing so. It is so necessary for my mental health.

I'm so glad I made this investment for my life. I'm reminded that as we build our careers and other things we desire in life, it's as important to build ourselves, discover ourselves, accept ourselves, love, cherish, honor and adore ourselves. Exercise has taught me how to be in tune with my body. When the body needs rest, you've got to listen to it. When you're stressed, your body will tell to you and often we ignore it. The more I maintain feeding and building my body and mind, I feel better about my life and everything that surrounds it, good or bad. It's mind over matter, I win every time and every time I will win. There will always be experiences, but they will never define me but remind me that I always overcome.

I'm empowered and in control of my health. It's helped me recognize the dark places and avoid welcoming it back in my space. When I experience what may be a dark place, I remember that I am the light and I have already overcome it. It's time to make some additional life changing decisions and there is no looking back." By this time, I had filed for divorce.

When my health began to decline, I knew I had to do something different.

While the affair was happening, I didn't utter a word to my husband or to her about what I knew. I gathered what was given to me and kept it moving.

There were some that knew before I did and thought I deserved such treatment. I call them mentally disturbed, hateful, and jealous because they knew nothing about me. Many of them claimed to be a part of the body of Christ and I had seen this narrative numerous times, so I was unbothered. It was quite hilarious to me.

There were no more questions to ask, no more conversations to be had, no more waiting for change, I had to be the change I wanted to see. Though it was still extremely hard to go through the process, I made up in my mind that I deserved so much more. As I reflected on who I knew God to be, I knew with my whole heart that God never desired for me to live, in no aspect of life in misery and pain. I didn't doubt God's ability to save my marriage, but I knew it was over for me. Enduring more pain to wait for change was not a risk I was willing to take. When you know it's over, you just know. No human on earth was going to convince me to change my mind about what I had to do for me.

I had to look at the pain people caused me from another perspective.

The reality was they were not doing anything to me but for me. It was all for my greater good. If you are married and miserable, God does not want you living this way. When you and your spouse began to head In two separate directions, you must focus on changing you and not the situation. Your religion can not save your marriage. Restoration is very possible but that's if both of you want it. It's called dual responsibility.

I don't care how much your spouse apologizes, if there are no evident, consistent actions showing that they are turning away from things that jeopardize your marriage, do yourself, your children a favor and do what's necessary for your peace. Trust God because he's the only source of your provision. The longer you stay, you will risk compromising the health of your entire being and your loved ones. You deserve better and you must understand and accept that truth. Journal entry: May 1, 2019, "I'm reminded to never be afraid to go through a separation that God is doing in your life. It's going to be extremely different because there's a ripping away of things that you've grown to live with and accept, but when you began to understand the deep love God has for you, the heart of God is for you to live free, to be yourself, to live life without reservations, to live in harmony with everyone he divinely sets in your life.

On the other side of the process is something that I would have never ever imagined or put together myself. He's preparing me for greater, my best, the blessings that make me rich and there's no sorrows added. Trust his wisdom, trust his will, trust his perfect way. He'll do it if I let him. I'm finally ready for this, raising my trust and faith in God because it's necessary for my new journey. "

Reflections

CHAPTER 5

Staying the Course

I'm still in the game but I have no idea of what's next.

Frightened, I still trust him, confused, I still trust him, humiliated and embarrassed, I still trust him. Feeling alone and no one can understand the sting of my situation, I still trust him. I am so desperate for a word of instruction, is it coming? I still trust him. When you are down to nothing and you sacrifice to follow what you know God has on the other side for you, you must have a stubborn determination to stand, be unmovable, steadfast, and focused, no matter what it looks and feels like.

Just because you tell God yes doesn't mean you won't feel the multiple bumps along the journey, but God has given you a memorable anchor. Your anchor could be that you are reminded of how he's kept you in years past.

The anchor could be a word you remember him speaking to you and it gives you comfort every time you think about it. Your anchor maybe a call from friends and family out of the blue to let you know that they are praying for you or just thinking of you when you drop in their spirit. Your anchor could be that scripture that always gives you that reminder that all things are working for you and not against you.

My brother, my sister I've never had my faith tested on this level before. I knew I was on the right path because it was so very uncomfortable in that new space.

Journal entry: June 14, 2019," So I run with God, not looking back, not hoping for what was because what was can never be again. The quality of life I'm headed into requires a new mindset and environment.

I choose the way of peace, the way that's full of love and light. The way that leads me into a greater awareness of who I am. These are confirmed instructions for me in this season. I choose to affirm who I am in God, this is my inheritance because I've been chosen and found worthy of all things abundant and serves my greater good, my children, friends and family. I've got to sit securely in the seat of this truth, be aggressive about it, invest in it, practice it, live it, breathe it, eat it, sleep it. This has got to be the appetite for this journey."

Journal entry July 13, 2019, "today I began a small fast, the past week or so has been very interesting, challenging, and intense mentally. I see why God said to worship, it's a must to keep the peace and maintain a grateful heart.

This has been the most peaceful I've been in years. It feels so good. I was thinking about where I used to be, tired and extremely exhausted, I felt desolate. I thought I would never get out of my situation but there always was an answer, I had to be mentally prepared for it. God knew when I was ready to take the leap with him. Just as he led so many out of darkness, he was doing the same for me."

Reflections

CHAPTER 6

Activation

Journal entry: August 19, 2019. "I'm feeling better mentally and physically, my hunger for the things that the world can't give me is increasing. It's a desire for the abundant life. I must take my faith to a higher place. I keep hearing "greater faith". Lord, it's bigger than what my eyes can see but I believe these things are available to me and my kids. Lord lead me deeper. Continue to set me apart and be ever so near to me. You've already shown me constant miracles, signs, and wonders. I know this is you showing me the compassion and love that I've always had access to and deserved. You give me gifts and surprises because I'm worthy of it. I can never do life without you." Have you ever been confused about your life? Have you made some poor decisions along your life's journey because you didn't understand your identity, but you kept your face turned to God? I want you to know that if you maintain that position, life won't have to be hard. He's going to keep you in perfect peace but you've got to decide to keep your mind stayed on who you know God is.

You must never deviate from that truth.

Just as your body needs food to survive, your mind and spirit needs positive words, positive atmospheres and environments that nurture you every day. No matter what, you've got to protect that space. To avoid even more frustration don't go trying to figure God out because it doesn't work.

Trust the timing of God because he is never wrong and has precise timing.

Journal Entry August 25, 2019," as I was in prayer and meditation this morning I felt very heavy. Instead of writing in my journal first, I began to pray. I know Holy Spirit said something very settling this morning that gave me peace. He said that "he is fulfilling the will of God on my life". Everything that I've experienced, good and bad has been a part of the plan. I belong to him, I have no reason to fear what's to come. Trust him in the journey, thank him in the journey, pursue him in the journey, watch and pray in the journey. He is doing the work so stay available, you've been set on his timetable."

Journal entry August 27, 2019 "God didn't bring you this far to leave you.

Since last week I've been feeling very heavy. I've made this harder than it has to be. I need more details God. I'm so scared to make the wrong moves. I've got to keep the faith and pray. God I don't like where I am mentally.

Maybe I just need to rest." During this journal entry I had begun making some moves but they were tiny steps that weren't showing any results. I couldn't understand why I felt so stagnant. In all actuality I was being impatient, I had to surrender to the process because God wasn't changing his mind. I had no choice but to give it all to God and not be swift to make things happen on my own. I vowed to God when I began my process that he had free rein to do what was necessary to carry me through and out. I had to remember that vow.

Reflections

CHAPTER 7

Another Level

Journal entry August 29, 2019 "In the blindness God is calling me to gain spiritual stability and insight. God wants me to work diligently in my spirituality, this is where I will find contentment while he's working on my behalf. God, I don't even see how I'm maintaining my sanity through this. I had a talk with a dear friend of mine about my situation, she reminded me to go through it well. Be honorable to God and maintain an attitude of gratefulness." Have I failed at this several times? Yes, yes, and yes! It has been challenging but I refused to follow through with what my flesh wanted.

Journal entry September 3, 2019" (Healed Blind) God is healing me from my traumas. I'm sure of it. I'm looking myself in the mirror and just amazed at how far I've come.

I have a crazy peace and a heart of thanksgiving that is so unreal. God saved my life. My life is a testimony of the great love God has for me. While I'm still waiting for this season of trials and test to pass, I can truly say I've learned so much about what's inside of me. I have no choice but to trust my redeemer.

My desire is to give my all to God; mind, body, and soul for what he's done in me and for me. I owe him my everything. I'll never forget the dark place, that empty and lonely place but more so, I'll never forget how God has restored me. This feels amazing, I'm being healed blind." God was doing something miraculous in my inner man.

These encounters with God filled me with hope and reminded me that my life was is his hands. I can't tell you all the intricacies of my transformation, all I know is when I began letting go of everything I knew, God began replacing those empty places with what I needed to move me further into what he desired for my life. Things that I've always deserved. I deserve love in all its different forms, whether it was loving on me more each day, valuing who I am and the value I bring to others, love from family. Having a romantic relationship where both of us enhance, elevate, celebrate, and bring peace to each other. I deserve as much money as I want, "Matthew 9:29 (MSG), become what you believe, it will happen." I deserve abundant life; I deserve the opportunity to change the world for the better because I'm working to achieve it. I have a choice of who I want in my circle and who's not allowed in it. I can choose what type of soil I drop my good seeds into, whether that's time, money, conversations. I choose to defy every odd set against me and even the ones that try to rise in my thoughts. I have the power to say "let me think about that", before I say yes or no to what someone is asking me to do. I have a choice to entertain certain conversations and not feel bad if someone is offended if I don't engage in it.

Being unbothered by the unproductive opinions of others will save you from delaying your purpose.

Reflections

33

CHAPTER 8

Unlearning

Journal entry: October 29, 2019 "As much as I thought I knew the pattern of life through reading the bible, listening to teachings, my own meditations and analyzing so much through this "unknowing" it's raised so many questions for me. I realize how much time I didn't give myself in cultivating my adulthood and allowing God to mold me. The emotions that I suppressed for so long began to rise to the surface. I thought I had a good understanding of how life was supposed to unfold, but being completely vulnerable to God, I've got a lot of unlearning to do. This new journey has taught me that it's impossible to pinpoint and know every "why" to a situation. All I know to do now is maintain my awareness for where I am, not deny it and present who I am now to God daily. The only person that really knows me is God, this knowledge is the only thing that allows me to be honest with him. He even knows the secret whispers of my heart. I know that if no one else hears and understands, I know that indeed he knows it." Through these last couple of journal entries, you can see that I am on a roller coaster of thoughts, feelings and emotions. Even though I was rising out of the dark, I also felt like there was no progression, no matter what I was doing. I wanted things to begin moving in a different and better direction quickly.

No one knows how long a season can take but God. The "wait" and when God begins to transform your life can seem life forever! I was always wrestling in my mind yet my yes was yes. You can never manipulate God into him giving you what you want. It does not work. When your adamant about rushing through the process God will sometimes give you what you want. Nine times out of ten, that thing you wanted doesn't amount to the value you thought it would add to your life.

Sometimes it could very well be that you're not ready to take on this new thing that you desire. Most of the time we don't even take the time to evaluate why we're wanting this thing or person so bad. We'd save ourselves a lot of trouble if we would put that necessary step into practice. Speaking from my experience, it's never God's style to go against my will.

It's better to go through the process and not focus on when the process is going to be over. It's almost like going in for a major surgery that lasts for several hours and could turn into a series of surgeries over a period of years. After the surgery, you go through the healing and recovery stage which can take an extensive amount of time. You can't expedite your healing, especially when you've had an unhealthy mindset the majority of your life. I allowed God to give me enlightenment on what was necessary for me to experience a fulfilling and abundant life. I knew I couldn't have that by staying in a toxic environment and being connected to toxic people.

Reflections

CHAPTER 9

Waiting

Journal Entry: January 27, 2020 Proverbs 19:21 (MSG) "Many plans are in a man's mind, but it is the Lord's purpose for him that will stand (be carried out)". This scripture has played a major role in my life journey. I've tried numerous times to make things happen because I was being impatient.

All I wanted to know was what was taking God so long to end this dread in my life, but I always found myself telling God that I would continue to wait because what he was doing for me I knew was worth the wait. Jeremiah 29:11 (MSG), "I know what I'm doing. I have it all planned out-plans to take care of you, not abandon you, plans to give you the future you hope for." His plan will always bring perfect fulfillment, meaning, sustainability and lasting fruit. I want to live God's truth for My life." I was being desperate, wanting a magical miracle to happen overnight.

Waiting never felt good to me, especially when I felt like I could make things happen faster on my own. Maybe you've found yourself in these same shoes and remember rushing ahead of God to get things done and it didn't turn out how you planned. Changing our perspective on waiting can be one of the greatest blessings of our lives. I knew that moving forward with my own agenda was not an option for me, so if I had to have a temper tantrum and cry it out, I was going to do that. I had specific instructions from God not to move and I was not going to go against that.

Journal entry: December 16, 2021 "Today I find myself growing more curious of the world and what's around me, engaging my thoughts more and what I believe about so many things. No new details from God on what's next and I know he's always saying something, I think he's just chosen not to say anything to me." At one point during this journey, back in 2017 I went to the extent of driving two hours to demand a word from God. I'll never forget that day. I remember getting on the road, I had an excruciating headache. On the way there, I said to God "Now God, I'm exercising my faith and I'm expecting this man of God to call me out of the crowd and give me some direction". I remember stating with so much conviction that I needed God to answer my prayer and I refused to accept anything else.

I had put a demand on God. I was very sure and excited to finally be in the atmosphere of this great prophet. When I arrived, there I was standing alone in this long line of people waiting to get into this service, anticipating the word he was going to release.

Surely, this was the night of "breakthrough". God I will be so happy to get some direction so that I feel like I'm at least getting somewhere. The service finally starts, the intercessor begins praying, I'm still begging God to please answer me, I didn't drive all this way in vain. I feel like you're going to honor my request. As the service progressed, here comes the man of God, he begins preaching and now he's beginning to step off the stage and into the crowd, my head was still pounding; my body was so tense from the stress of the day and I knew he was coming near me. He was calling people out from the right and left giving the word of the Lord, the closer he gets, I'm praying, "God, let him see me, please don't let him pass without my word". He's getting closer and looks in my direction, it appeared that he looked me in my eyes just for a moment. In my head I was thinking, "Finally, it's my time", after that , he turned his head and proceeded to the back of the church. My heart sunk, I was heartbroken.

He never summoned me over to receive a word. I was utterly disappointed, angry, crying. This can't be happening; I drove this far and God you knew what I needed, and you did not honor My request. I was pissed. As the prophet made his way back to the front, he got the microphone and stated to the audience, "some of you need to get acquainted with the voice of God". At that moment, I knew that was for me. My head dropped; I knew what that meant for me. Apparently, I wasn't the only one that needed that word.

As I began to process that moment, I began to ask God, isn't my situation deemed an emergency to you? Don't you see how much pain I'm in? God I can't bear this! I can't even focus enough right now to even hear for myself! God was not going to do what I wanted just because I was extremely irritated and uncomfortable. He understood exactly where I was. It was like he was telling me you're okay and you're going to learn who I am to you, my way.

In all actuality, God answered me and that meant having to accept that he was not going to allow other individuals to participate in what he was going to perform for my life. He was going to get all the glory.

It seemed like too much work to hear God's voice, my mind was so cluttered with everything else, how did God expect me to focus on that when I couldn't even trust whether I was hearing him or not. It seemed like I had been at war alone, I was completely exhausted because I couldn't be still in my mind.

God wasn't looking for me to do anything but trust him and allow him to fight for me. That was all he required of me.

Reflections

CHAPTER 10

Spiritual Maintenance

As I have been writing for years, God has been speaking and encouraging me through my writings. I didn't realize it until later. God can never be placed in box. He can use any resource to get your attention. It's masterfully different for everyone. Over the course of reading my own journal entries, I saw God speaking to me throughout the pages. As I was writing down my thoughts, God begin to speak through my pen. It was him because some of the writings didn't sound like me at all, but it was. It was the God in me.

God has been the ultimate gentleman to me; I can't even begin to tell you how patient and longsuffering he's been. I don't have an explanation for all the twists and turns that have taken place so far. I don't have a three step process to share with you. One major lesson I've learned is no matter how horrible the mistakes I've made and continue to make, I stay true to God and who Brandy is, flaws and all. God will always be my help in the time of trouble and triumph. When I keep my mind stayed on all the many things he's brought me through, I have no room to be ungrateful or feel forsaken, because I'm not. All of us are on a spiritual journey and no one has the same order of going through it.

God engages with each of us differently. The journal entries that you've read so far is a depiction of what most of us do when God is taking us through and out of situations and mindsets that don't nurture us into wholeness and a fulfilling life.

This was an agonizing, wilderness experience for me but it turned into one of the most beautiful experiences I've ever had with God. You would think that I would be done dealing with people because of all the craziness that I went through but my life is not based on as long as I have King Jesus, I don't need nobody else. This experience has given me the power of compassion and the power to forgive. When you see those that you loved hurt you the most move forward seemingly living their best lives and don't feel any remorse for what they've done to you, it becomes a complete illusion we create in our own minds that their wickedness is triumphing over us.

Please trust, believe, know with everything that's' in you that it is a complete smoke screen to throw you off course and make you feel like you've got to intervene and do something about it. The reality is you are doing something about it, you are surrendering to the master vindicator. I refused to activate revenge techniques that I used in the past. I was a different woman this time around. I told God that I was ready to be vindicated by him but had no idea how he was going to do it.

I could not afford to renege on what I requested of God. Any move made on my own volition was not going to get me long lasting results.

Besides, what I was facing was way bigger than me and God knew it through and through. This was the year that my divorce was supposed to be finalized but that did not happen. Who could ever forget the year of Covid- 19. More unexpected adjustments and once again I felt like everything was put on pause but had no idea it would be another year. I began working from home while the kids began school virtually. I was grateful to at least be separated and I knew it was necessary to take advantage of this time. None of this happened by coincidence. I was either going to catch on to what God wanted to do with me or set myself farther back by not complying to the shift that was getting ready to take place. Even though the divorce was suspended due to the pandemic, I resolved that God was still at work on my behalf, there was still some exposure that needed to happen. The affair was still in full effect, during the time George Floyd was murdered, my husband and his mistress coordinated and led a black lives matter march in the same town we all lived in. At that moment I knew that there was a mental disconnect somewhere in both of them. It was astonishing to watch. I believe God allowed me to see all these things because he knew I could handle it and it was about getting things done for me to exit out of Egypt.

I was what you call, thug'in it out. I felt nothing while watching everything play out.

I couldn't mark my point of growth but I knew something had drastically changed within me. Even though my mood was not the best every day, I found myself saying "God, my answer is still and will always be yes".

Reflections

CHAPTER 11

The Tide is Turning

I learned so much about God and myself during 2020. Instead of complaining I saw the opportunity to rediscover who God really was to me. I received so many love messages from God. I would be taking a walk outside and all of a sudden this amazing breeze would rush over me, I learned how to stop and feel his presence even in the wind, I cannot express how amazing that felt but I wanted to acknowledge God by telling him thank you when I was aware of those endearing moments. I realized that I could have this every day for the rest of my life if I choose to receive it. I knew that the blessings before me were going to be nothing short of mind blowing.

Everything that took place for me in 2020 and prior was the gateway to what was getting ready to open up for me in 2021.

Journal entry July 31, 2021," I've been in deep reflection these few weeks and I've been listening to some deep, thought- provoking teachings that have given me a whole new perspective on my spiritual journey.

My heart is wide open. I feel like the abundant life I've been desiring for years is now upon me. I just believe that the coming years are going to be the best years of my life." Journal entry 8/2/2021:" For several weeks now, I have been on a search. Searching for answers and what to do next. I already know God has things set for me. How it will happen is still a mystery.

As God carries me in silence in this season, I will continue to follow his orders.

I am certain the outcome will be great and grand."

Journal entry September 2, 2021: "I will not forget you". Everything that became first in my life became last as God began to remove every layer that was preventing me from thriving like he wanted me to. This month I'm believing God as I go through this process. I'm all in with God on this. I'm learning, still learning." Something indescribable was happening inside me. My mind was expanding in ways that I couldn't explain. The more I let my resistance down, the more God was pouring in me, the more he revealed me to me. He showed me my growth, he showed me that he could trust me with the information that was given to me, he showed me that I had a stubborn determination. I was not going to let anyone or anything change my mind about moving forward in what I had to do for my life. What is it that holds you back from pursuing a greater wholistic view of yourself? Are you afraid of what people may say? Does it have to make sense before you bust a move? How long will you stay in a place that doesn't promote your growth and well-being? I loved what seemed like stability but that level of comfort wasn't profiting me or increasing my faith. If the events that took place in my life did not happen, I would not be where I am today. The testing of your faith is life altering, that's what it's supposed to do. It's supposed to take you from faith to faith and glory to glory.

None of it is ever comfortable but if you know God and have had encounters with him, you've got to lean on that until you get to the other side. Don't forfeit your promise land because you've gotten comfortable in your "stability".

There's more for you to gain and become.

Reflections

CHAPTER 12

First class seat to destiny

In the month of September 2021, I decided to go on a fast. So much was happening within me and my desire was to focus on what God wanted me to understand. I learned over time that fasting was a powerful weapon that always worked for me. When I felt like my emotions were all over the place, I could quiet the busyness of my mind by fasting. Fasting allows me to be intentional about filtering out negative thoughts and replacing them with positive ones. It allows me to remember who I am, and the power I possess. This is one of the ways I receive enlightenment and empowerment.

The year 2014, everything that I thought was under control, slipped through my fingers. I had never felt so naked before God. I knew that I could not reach back to what was. I had to move without ever having the thought of looking back. I knew that my trust in God was going to give me long lasting, life changing results that would not be denied if I followed his leading. Journal entry September 7, 2021: "My first day of fasting and I'm doing well. The week of Rosh Hashanah, the Hebrew new year. God is going to do something big! I'm getting ready to walk into promise. I want to take these next three days to open my ears and hear what God is saying to me. I believe I'm finally, after all these years where God wants me to be. Right now, I need strength, courage and faith. I know God is going to do it, it's just a matter of time.

Things I want to take away from this time of fasting is a keener ear to God's voice, direction for me and my kids, a new level of knowledge of him and a stronger relationship with him, financial guidance, and wisdom. Wisdom for my house on what's to come, new mind shift and being open to what God wants to do during this time of fasting and prayer. I will please God with my faith. God help me to unlearn what was complete error, I'm open to this. I'm aware that there's a lot I do, think, and say that puts me in my own ignorant bondage. Help me to understand what I've been missing my entire life. This is my desire. Open my mind and heart to this." In that moment, I knew I was ready to be a student of the Most High, I had graduated to a new level. God knew that I was ready, and I knew I was ready to go deeper. Going deeper was very cliché in church. We would sing about it, pray and preach about it but had no idea what we were asking God. From the condition of most of our lives, we were not ready for that journey. I believe it was a honest desire for many of us but the disconnect was the lack of knowledge and commitment to follow through. For me, many times it was an emotional moment I constantly had in church service, only to go home in the same state of mind that I came to church with. I knew that there was something more but had no idea how to obtain it. Journal entry September 9/11/2021: "This fast gave me a new appetite. Wow what transpired over the course of a day of fasting turned into a hunger for the truth, wisdom, understanding and being open to what God needed to show me. Fasting this time around gave me a hunger and appetite for something my entire being had never experienced before. Going beyond the bible. I'm finally realizing how much of a spirit being I am. This revelation is getting ready to take me places I never thought I would go." Journal entry September 13, 2021, "things are beginning to stir a little more. My mind has been going a million miles an hour about the freedom God has given me. It's messing me up in a good way and shaking up all of what I thought I knew. This is taking my thinking to another place."

Reflections

CHAPTER 13

Sentenced to life

It is still the year 2021 and I have not finalized my divorce, but I have taken on a new paradigm of my life, I'm completely transformed in my mind.

Journal entry October 24, 2021: "It's a spiritual awakening that's been taken place for the last few months. I've been led by God to begin a journey of more in depth self-discovery and what that looks like for me. It has been confirmed that God desires for me to live an abundant life and it starts with self awareness. It is no longer necessary to use the bible as my only resource on this journey, dive into more resources and tap into the spirit world and discover the beauty, the unlimited power and access that I have to create the life I've always imagined." Using this type of language was extremely uneasy for me.

Coming from a religious background, this is considered blasphemy and evil in some religious spaces. When I realized that God desired this for me and I began to meditate on that truth, it was as if all of my fears of going to hell for thinking this way dissolved. I was truly born again in the most amazing way. This felt different than any church experience I had encountered. Although going to church brought about some amazing things for me and established a lot of my foundation, there was more to my life that I had yet to discover. God had sentenced me to life, to live in a way that brought me everything my heart could desire. To be love and light to the world that needs me so desperately. This is living, to walk boldly in my spiritual authority without reservations. This was God's gift to me. To have his image and likeness. To operate in my God conscious for the rest of my days and show my children the way. I know now that this is the way to be the generational curse breaker for my family. I am Isaiah 61. I am anointed for this and God approves my message. The month of September my only brother passed away. It was a shocking and devastating time for my family. I was blessed to have even taken on a new perspective of death while going through my spiritual awakening. I know that my brother is not dead but has taken on the fullest true form of himself in the spirit, he is more alive than ever before watching over me and my family. When I viewed his body in the casket, he looked so handsome and at peace. I've never seen my brother look so well. I look at my son and he's the splitting image of my brother. I know that there is so much purpose behind what's happening and it's all working out for the good of my life and the life of my children."

Reflections

CHAPTER 14

Surrender

It's the year 2022, I'm finally divorced as of January 25, 2022. The wait was more than worth it. My commitment to follow through with the instructions God gave me has paid off in a tremendous way.

Patience has been my virtue. I know that I am being rewarded and vindicated by God because I chose to stay the course during the process. I do not celebrate divorce at all, but what I do celebrate and honor myself for is knowing that I was worthy of so much better. I decided to take a quantum leap to change my life and the life of my kids forever. One major lesson learned in the process is learning how to surrender all to God. I understand this to mean for me that I can no longer be in a state of resistance with God. There so many scriptures that reference letting go, releasing worry and trusting God. Can you imagine what that feels like? Just letting go? Letting go of what people think of you, letting go of all obligations we often stress about, letting go of hurt, disappointment, and everything that causes us to not enjoy life the way that God intended? My strongest, sincerest prayer for you that are reading is to discover the unique relationship you have with your Creator.

There are so many unlimited areas of your life to discover that he's place on the inside of you. God wants to give you the world. You were made in his image and likeness which means that you are just like him.

Many of us can't take that on as the reality because of how we were taught and could never fathom ourselves as just like him. Many of us believe that God is separated from us, he's holy and we are not, he's powerful and we are not. Many of us pray, declare and decree but subconsciously we don't believe in any of what we're saying and we say it in the fear of what could happen. We do it all the time. When we get bad news, we want to pray, but we pray in fear, think about that.

Ask yourself this question, what would it truly feel like to completely fall into the safety of Gods arms from here, until. I'll tell you as a person doing it now it is what my whole life has been waiting for.

My challenge to you after reading this book is to find new ways to connect with God. Maybe just opening your heart to him to unlearn what's held you in your own bondage. Free yourself with the truth of who he really is and who you really are. You will be so amazed at what you discover, he'll gently lead you through it, if you allow him. Change can be extremely nerve recking. You want to make sure, you're making the right decisions and not messing your life up more than what it already is. When the things and people in your life are not moving you into a place of excelling in your worth and value but damaging you from the inside out, don't worry about making the wrong moves and separating yourself from what you know is tearing you apart. Make the move and trust God. God has done it for me time and time again. There were plenty of times I didn't even know I was in a toxic place, God took me out without my permission. It was devastating and I was angry with God but the more I stayed out of that toxic place he took me out of, I could see from the outside how unhealthy that place was.

Even though I felt alone, God was with me. When I was finally tired of going through the same cycle year in and year out, I took the risk. When I let go, and came to the end of myself, God began cutting off everything that was not fruitful for my life. I cried, I had temper tantrums, I fussed at God, I wrestled with him, I wanted to quit, but I knew God didn't bring me this far to leave me. The story of my abundant life is just beginning. I've made it through the doors of my promise land.

Nothing and no one can stop what God has already set out for me to have.

When you are truly ready to move to the next level of knowing, God is always ready to move you forward.

Remember this famous quote by Buddha Siddhartha Guatama Shakyamuni, that goes: When the student is ready, the teacher will appear.

To God be the glory!

Brandy Simmons

Reflections

My Mental Health Practices

Going into nature

- ♦ This helps to clear my mind and focus on gratitude. I'm able to reflect on the amazing love of God, his creation, feel his presence, and recharge. One of my favorite places is near the water.

Encouraging others

- ♦ This is a major staple in my life. Naturally I'm a giver and love serving others. This helps me to stay focused on the goodness and love of God by sharing an encouraging word. Reminding them that they are not alone, and reminding them that they are always in my prayers, and I have their back. Just about every time I've done this that person needed that check-in I was giving, and vise versa.

Giving

- ♦ giving allows me to forget about what's going on in my life to serve someone who maybe experiencing a harder times. This helps me to show the love of God and maintain gratitude in my life.

Playing my favorite jams and dancing

- ◆ I love music, I see it as a great way to medicate my mind, body and soul when I don't feel the best. Movement and being in the moment helps to lift my spirit and recharge.

Journaling

- ◆ this is my time pour out everything in my mind, organized and not so organized. It's a judge free zone for me and it allows God space to write through me and receive enlightenment. It helps to clear my head of negative thoughts, encourage myself and write down everything I see that I desire for my life. It also provides me with wisdom.

Exercise

- ◆ Naturally exercise releases endorphins in your body that make you feel amazing and positive, this is the feeling I get every time, alongside feeling like I can conquer the world and everything in it.

Reading a book

- ◆ Allows me time to think and process what the author is saying. Helps me to maintain focus. How I can gain a better understanding of life, history, and new things I can put in place to enhance my own life.

Learning a new word

♦ This helps me to learn more ways to articulate my feelings and communicate more effectively with others. It empowers me.

Going out by myself and intentionally meeting new people

♦ If you've never tried this you should, most of the time, I'm the one introducing myself but, in the end, I meet people and get to hear some of their stories. This is very rewarding for me and helps me to see how big and beautiful this life is.

Laughter

♦ The Bible mentions laughter several times and how soothing it is for the soul, it does just that for me. It's very challenging to feel depressed and negative when you practice laughter, it's great medicine for the whole body.

Meditation/Prayer/Fasting

♦ It took some time for me to learn what works best for me in meditation but I'm constantly learning. Affirming who I am and who I am in God. Finding something to be grateful and thankful for. Smiling while I think on things that are good and the goodness of God, thanking God for others while I meditate, taking deep breathes and really focusing on nothing else but the moment of silence and peace, letting go and releasing fears and replacing them with words that empower me, thinking on all the promises of God. Fasting helps me to submit my body to God and remind my body of who is in charge. It's a powerful tool and a great way to edify your mind, body, and spirit.

Forgiveness

- Forgiving myself for my mistakes and reaffirming who I am. When I think of those that have done me harm, I pray sincerely for them and bless their lives. I've found that it takes too much energy to hate and be bitter towards people. I will not die sick because I couldn't let people go but will live the long satisfying life God promised me. I've been open to God concerning this area of my life, he has allowed me to grow into having this uncommon love for people. I'm grateful for it and will forever cherish this gift.

About the Author

Brandy Simmons was born and raised in Florence, S.C. where she resided with her mother. Once she graduated from Wilson High School, she began undergrad at Coker College in Hartsville, S.C. where she earned a degree in Business Administration and a minor in voice. She has three children, her son and twin daughters. She loves serving, singing, dancing, getting to know new people, sharing the love of God with others, fashion, traveling, reading, eating and enjoying this new, authentic life God has introduced her to and has divinely called her to live out.